Really Short Walks
in North Devon

Robert Hesketh

Bossiney Books · Launceston

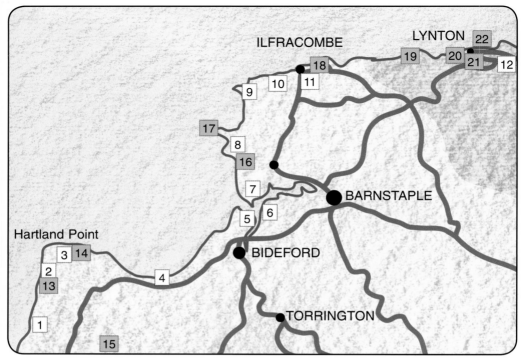

The approximate locations of the walks in this book

All the walks in this book were checked prior to publication, at which time the instructions were correct. However, changes can occur in the countryside over which neither the author nor publisher has any control. Please let us know if you encounter any serious problems.

First published 2010 by
Bossiney Books Ltd, Langore, Launceston, Cornwall PL15 8LD
www.bossineybooks.com

ISBN 978-1906474-19-5

Acknowledgements
The maps are by Nick Hawken
Cover based on a design by Heards Design Partnership
All photographs are by the author or from the publisher's own collection.

Printed in Great Britain by R Booth Ltd, Penryn, Cornwall

Introduction

The walks in this book are mostly 3-5km (2-3 miles) in length. Some are easy, others short but challenging. All have been chosen to show north Devon's unparalleled scenery – cliffs and beaches, woodland, waterfalls and rivers.

We have not suggested how long they will take, because these routes offer many wonderful viewpoints and places of interest to linger over, and because some people walk faster than others.

Clothing and footwear

Do go prepared. Devon's weather can change rapidly, and even within a short walk there may be a considerable temperature difference when you climb from a sheltered valley to a cliff top exposed to a sea breeze. Always carry extra layers of clothing as well as a waterproof. On some paths, especially inland, you are likely to come across briars, thorns and nettles, so bare legs can be a liability.

There will be some mud at most times of the year and perhaps a lot of mud and puddles in winter or after a wet spell. Ideally, therefore, wear walking boots – and certainly not sandals! Wellington boots are not recommended, as they don't breathe or provide ankle support. I find a walking pole is a considerable help. It is sensible to carry water, as dehydration causes tiredness.

Safety

Please watch out for uneven ground, especially on the coast path, and keep clear of the cliff edge because it is not fenced off from the drop. Take special care when the path does take you near the edge: go no nearer than you have to and keep a close eye on children and dogs. The sketch maps in this book are just that – sketches. You may want to carry an OS 1:25,000 map for extra information.

The countryside

Despite many pressures on their livelihoods, farmers are still trying to make a living from the land you will pass through. Please respect their crops. Leave gates closed or open as you find them, and keep dogs under control, especially during the lambing and bird nesting season.

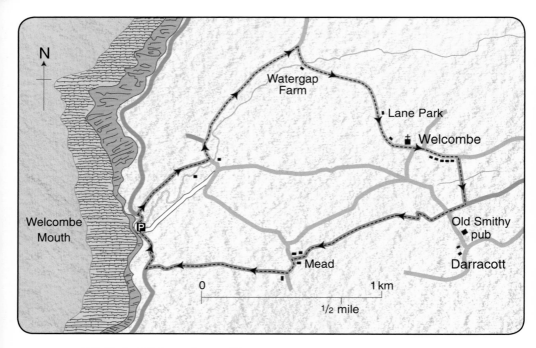

Walk 1 Welcombe and Darracott

Distance: 5 km (3 miles)

Character: A mainly inland walk on footpaths and quiet lanes, but including the dramatic beach at Welcombe Mouth with its high cliffs, saw-toothed rocks and waterfall. One steep descent and one long steep ascent.

Starting point: The directions start from the National Trust car park at Welcombe Mouth, but access is by narrow lanes and a rough and narrow track. You may prefer to start from the small parking area by Welcombe church – though not when there's a service due, please. If you're lunching at the Old Smithy, you'll probably be allowed to walk from the car park there, but please ask first.

From the Welcombe Mouth car park: facing the beach, turn right and cross the stream by stepping stones. (If you don't fancy the stepping stones, you can walk back up the access track and turn left along the lane, see map.)

Pause to see the waterfall, then walk through the gap in the wall in front of the stepping stones. Turn right and follow the unsigned path which runs parallel to the stream, over heath and through a wood. Arriving at a lane, turn left and follow it to Watergap Cross.

4

Turn right, WELCOMBE, and follow the lane steeply uphill to St Nectan's church. This contains Devon's oldest carved screen as well as finely carved ceiling bosses and a Norman font.

Continue along the lane past the staggered crossroads and cottages. Turn right, PUBLIC FOOTPATH, and follow this down across a stream and up to a grassy track. Turn right.

On reaching a lane, either continue ahead, PUBLIC FOOTPATH, or divert left 150 m for refreshments at the Old Smithy, a 17th century building which became a pub in the early 1960s.

Return to the public footpath. Follow it between hedges and over a stream. Cross a stile and turn right, keeping the hedge on your right across three fields, then going through a converted farm complex to a lane. Turn left. When the lane turns sharp left after 100 m, turn right, PUBLIC FOOTPATH. This leads between hedges to a stile. Cross and walk ahead over fields towards the sea. Turn right onto the Coast Path and follow it steeply downhill to the car park.

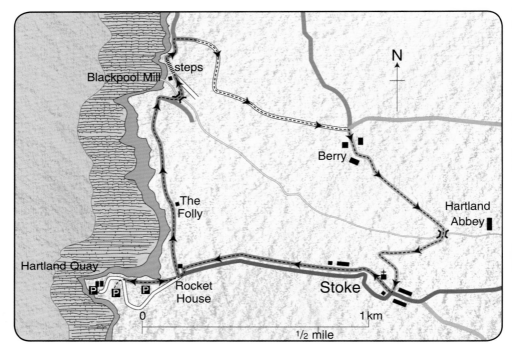

Walk 2 Hartland Quay and Stoke

Distance: 5.25 km (3 1/4 miles)
Character: Quite a strenuous walk with several steep ascents and descents, offering sweeping views of Devon's Atlantic coast and some especially dramatic rock formations.

Start from the middle level car park at Hartland Quay. Walk back up the tarmac track then bear left on a path directly up the hill to the Rocket House, where life saving gear was once stored. Turn left (COAST PATH HARTLAND POINT) and continue past the 'folly', a ruined tower, and down the main path keeping well clear of the unstable cliff edge.

The path descends then turns inland to a junction. Turn left, COAST PATH HARTLAND POINT. Turn left when you reach a track by Blackpool Mill, then right up the steps. At the top, turn right at a gate as signed, then left. After a short descent, turn right up a track, passing a house on your left. Follow the stony track out to a tarmac lane. Turn right, UNSUITABLE FOR MOTORS.

Follow the lane through Berry, then downhill, with the 39 m tower of Stoke church ahead of you – a landmark for shipping. At the bottom of the valley there's a fine view of Hartland Abbey and its park.

Consecrated in 1160, the abbey was dissolved in 1539 and sold off. The frontage you can see dates from a rebuilding in 1779.

Follow the lane as it winds up the far side of the valley. Near the top of the slope, turn right on the PUBLIC FOOTPATH which leads through the churchyard. At the end of the churchyard continue ahead, PUBLIC FOOTPATH. This runs parallel to the busy lane, past houses and on into a field. Keep the hedge on your left and you will arrive back at the Rocket House.

A short diversion downhill from the middle car park leads to the Quay, with its shop (seasonal), pub and hotel, offering a range of refreshments. Above the shop there is an excellent maritime museum.

Despite its exposed position, the quay continued in use from Queen Elizabeth's reign to the late 19th century, handling a variety of cargoes, including malt for the malt house and limestone to feed the three kilns. A small bank issued notes until 1833.

St Nectan's is worth seeing inside for its monuments and brasses and especially its wonderful ceiling and carved screen. The 'Pope's Chamber', which is reached by a small door in the north wall, is a miniature museum.

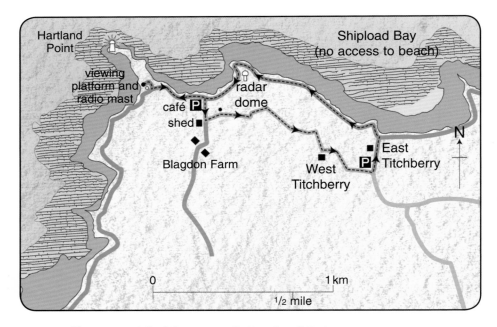

Walk 3   East Titchberry and Hartland Point

Distance: 4km (2¹/₂ miles)
Character: This dramatically beautiful walk is surprisingly gentle.
The Point, with its high cliffs and lighthouse, is at the junction between
the Atlantic and the Bristol Channel. Low tide reveals the 'Johanna':
one of a long line of wrecks, she came to grief in 1982.

Park in the National Trust's car park at East Titchberry, beside the
road out towards Hartland Point. From the top end of the car park,
turn left (COASTPATH BRIDLEWAY) passing the farmhouse to your left.
Turn left at the coast path, HARTLAND POINT.

Walk round the enclosure of the mushroom-shaped radar dome.
Built in 1994, this is the successor to the RAF's Hartland radar station,
which plotted shipping and aircraft during the Second World War and
for some time afterwards.

Arriving at the Hartland Point café and car park, continue ahead,
COASTPATH HARTLAND QUAY, towards the Point. Whilst there is a path
of sorts to the rocky end of the point, it is difficult and risky, so we
don't recommend it. There is a viewing point with a helpful information board, from which to look over the wild seascape.

Retrace your steps to the café. Turn right and follow the tarmac
track past the Lundy heliport. Turn left, PUBLIC BRIDLEWAY and walk

8

past the wooden hut. Follow the lane past West Titchberry to the starting point.

Hartland Point is a landmark for migrating birds, making visits in Autumn and Spring particularly interesting. Resident species include ravens, peregrines and (especially) buzzards.

The Point is also a favourite place for seals, which are most vocal in the breeding season, from September to December. Their calls, somewhere between a bark and a trumpet blast, are large and exuberant, like their generous waistlines. Mature males grow to over 2 m long and weigh in at well over 200 kg. Females average a modest 155 kg.

Hartland light was built in 1874 and manned until 1984. Alas, it did not save every vessel on this busy sea lane from running into the rocks, as *Johanna's* rusting carcass testifies. All her crew were safely brought to land by the rescue services, but they were less than pleased when the *Johanna's* cargo was later brought ashore – by looters.

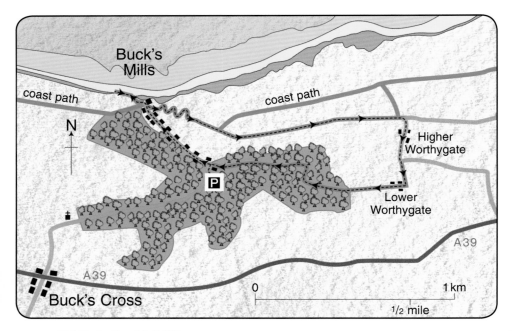

Walk 4 Buck's Mills

Distance: 3.4km (2 miles) or 3km without visiting the beach.
Character: An inland circuit through woods and fields from the pretty
fishing village of Buck's Mills. It involves one sharp ascent, or two if you
visit the beach. The diversion down to the rocky beach is richly repaid
with dramatic coastal views, fascinating rock strata and a waterfall,
as well as reminders of past industry – a quay, limekilns and rusting
winches.

Turn right out of the Buck's Mills car park and follow the lane downhill for 450 m to a red telephone booth (at the time of writing). You
could shorten the walk by turning right here at the COASTPATH sign.
Otherwise carry on steeply downhill to the beach.

Then retrace your steps to the telephone booth. Turn left, COASTPATH
PEPPERCOMBE. The path climbs steeply, with zig-zags and steps,
through trees – mainly oaks stunted by the salt winds. When you
reach a path junction, fork right, WORTHYGATE. Follow the enclosed
path. When it briefly opens up, look back for a great view of Clovelly
and Hartland Point. Arriving at a tarmac lane, turn right.

Walk past Higher Worthygate. Just after the lane turns sharp left, turn
right (PUBLIC FOOTPATH) to Lower Worthygate. Turn right (PUBLIC
FOOTPATH). Walk to the right of the farmhouse. Don't enter the field

Above: The rocks on Buck's Mills beach are folded and contorted layers of siltstone and shale, interbedded with harder layers of sandstone. They have eroded at different rates, producing the ridges characteristic of Devon's Atlantic coast

Below: From the village square

ahead of you. Walk up a shallow concrete ramp to a small gate to the left of a barn. Continue ahead, PUBLIC FOOTPATH, with the hedge on your left. Go through a metal gate and downhill through a wood.

On reaching a lane, turn left uphill to the car park.

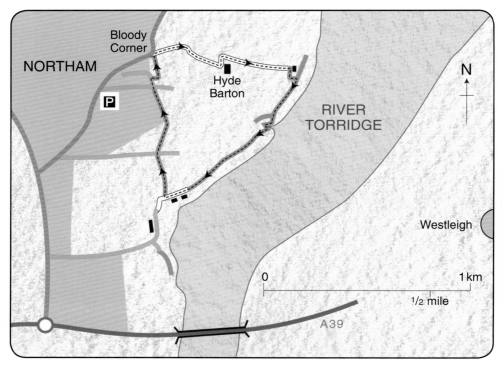

Walk 5 Bloody Corner, Northam

Distance: 2.5 km (1 1/2 miles)

Character: This fairly gentle walk mainly by riverbank and field paths offers splendid views of the river Torridge. It starts from the battle site of 878, when Devon men defeated a Viking host.

Getting there: From the roundabout on the A39 at Bideford, take the Northam road. After 0.7 km (nearly half a mile) turn right, APPLEDORE. Bloody Corner is 0.8 km (half a mile) towards Appledore, where the grass verge on the left broadens considerably. Park carefully by the roadside, or if there is no space, use the Windmill Lane car park 200 m back up the hill on the left.

From Bloody Corner take the tarred track ahead, a public footpath, HYDE BARTON. Follow the twists past Hyde Barton as far as a wooden gate signed BOAT HYDE AND THE MOORINGS.

Turn right over a stile, COAST PATH. This path leads to the riverbank, with good views of Westleigh and of Instow further downriver. Look out for and listen for wading birds.

Turn right and follow the path for about 100 m, then turn left (acorn sign, NATIONAL TRUST BOROUGH FARM).

Follow the bankside path over a small creek by duckboards. (If the tide is high, there is an alternative higher path which soon rejoins the main path.) Continue along a fenced section, with views upriver to the new road bridge and beyond.

Just before the track descends to the valley bottom, turn sharp right over a stile, PUBLIC FOOTPATH. Walk uphill past a tree plantation. Cross a tarmac track and a stile, continuing on the footpath with the hedge on your left. Do not turn into the housing estate, but continue along the fenced footpath to a street.

Turn left and immediately right down GREENHILL CLOSE, enjoying the sea view. After 50 m, turn right (PUBLIC FOOTPATH) at a metal gate, then turn left down the field edge to a metal gate at the bottom left corner. Turn left back to Bloody Corner.

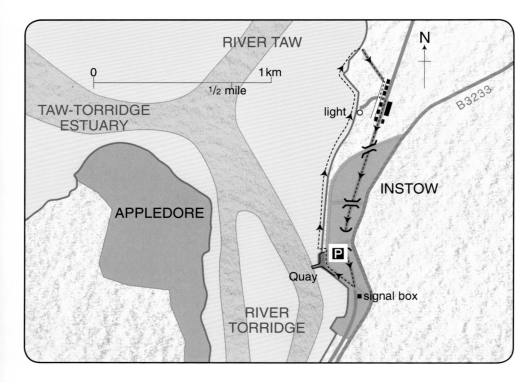

Walk 6   Instow

Distance: 3 km (2 miles) – less if you use the high tide short cut.
Character: A beautiful walk along Instow's sandy beach, with views across the estuary to Appledore and Braunton Burrows, is followed by an easy return along the Tarka Trail. Here the former railway line has been smoothly surfaced and is pushchair-friendly. The whole route is level.

From the signed car park on Instow's Marine Parade, turn right. After 75 m, leave the pavement at the beach kiosk and follow the top edge of the beach. Continue along the beach. leaving Instow behind you and keeping the dunes on your right.

On reaching the navigation light, you may wish to take a short cut on the right across MOD property and along the concrete track to a former level crossing. If the tide is very high, you may be obliged to do this. Ignore the next paragraph.

Otherwise, continue ahead with the sea wall on your right until you reach the COAST PATH sign. Turn right up the steps onto the sea wall.

Leaving the Coast Path, continue ahead (PUBLIC FOOTPATH) past a cricket pitch and thatched pavilion. Turn right along a metalled track past wooden chalets as far as the MOD concrete road and turn left.

Turn right at the former level crossing onto the Tarka Trail – beware cyclists! Continue to Instow signal box, which dates from 1872 and is a listed building. Preserved along with its levers, and short section of re-laid track and a working signal, it is open on Sunday afternoons.

Turn right and follow Marine Parade back to the car park.

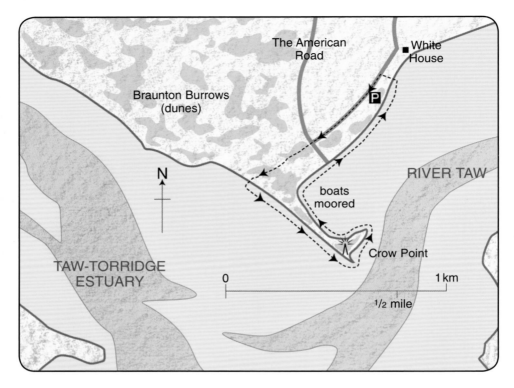

Walk 7 Crow Point and Braunton Burrows

Distance: 4km (2¹/₂ miles)

Character: A level and entirely off-road walk with impressive views from the massive sand dunes of Braunton Burrows to north Devon's Atlantic coast and the Taw-Torridge estuary. The Burrows' remarkable variety of wildflowers and birds provide added interest.

Getting there: From Braunton take the road signed to Crow Point. The latter part is a toll road, but with a modest toll and free parking.

Leave Crow Point car park from the western end (furthest from the toll road). Take the path between two large boulders beside a notice board which gives information on the Burrows' flora and fauna.

Warning

The Burrows are still used for military training. Although this does not directly affect this walk, do not pick up metal objects or enter areas of the Burrows marked off with red flags – which implies live firing.

Stay on the path when it crosses a rough track – the 'American Road'. (US troops trained in this area of north Devon as well as at Slapton on the south coast in preparation for D-Day, 1944.) Please stay on the duckboards to minimise erosion and damage to plants.

Arriving at the beach, turn left and walk along to Crow Point. Try to find the hardest sand to make the going easier! From Crow Point's red navigation light (private property belonging to Trinity House) follow the beach around the hook-shaped Point, keeping to the sand to avoid the sticky mud closer to the water line.

A variety of boats are moored in the lee of Crow Point. Ahead is the White House. Built for the marsh keeper, it was formerly known as Ferry House because a ferry ran from here to Appledore until 1939.

As you approach the White House, look out for a flight of metal steps. These lead back to the car park.

Braunton Burrows is a UNESCO Biosphere Reserve, renowned for its great diversity and wealth of flora. Over 400 species of flowering plants have been recorded here. The Burrows also support a strong butterfly population, whilst skylarks, whitethroats and stonechats are common. Look out for waders and heron on the marshes.

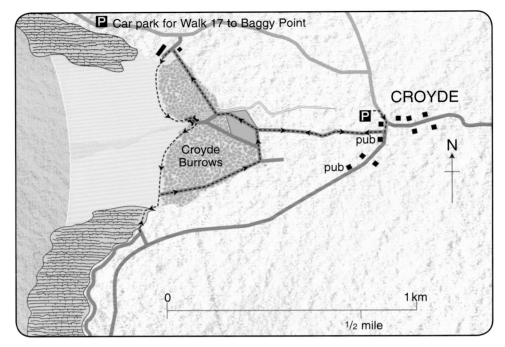

Car park for Walk 17 to Baggy Point

CROYDE

Croyde
Burrows

pub

pub

N

0   1 km

1/2 mile

Walk 8 Croyde Burrows

Distance: 4km (2 1/2 miles)

Character: Salt air and the roar of surf are the usual companions on this invigorating exploration of Croyde's large golden beach and sand dunes. The route is almost entirely off road and involves no steep slopes.

Start from Croyde's village hall car park. Turn right out of the car park and right again at Billy Budd's pub, PUBLIC FOOTPATH TO THE BEACH. Stay on the enclosed path until you reach a small meadow. Bear diagonally right.

Do not take the first path right, into the caravan park. Take the second right over a footbridge and into the dunes. Please stay with the path to minimise erosion and avoid adders, which like to bask in quiet spots on the sand. Dogs should be kept to the path.

On reaching the beach café, turn left and walk along the top edge of the beach – part of the official Coast Path – to a stream. Follow it inland to a footbridge and cross. Make your way along the far side of the stream and continue along the beach to a ramp at the far end. This leads through a cove to public steps at the far end of the beach. Climb these for superb views of Baggy Point and of the saw-toothed rocks leading to it.

Now return to the ramp and retrace your steps along the beach for 100m. Turn right at a wooden fingerpost (damaged at the time of writing) and walk up the dune to a large metal signboard. Continue inland along the sandy path through the dunes and past chalets to a junction of paths. Turn left. At the next path junction turn right, cross the meadow and retrace your steps to the start.

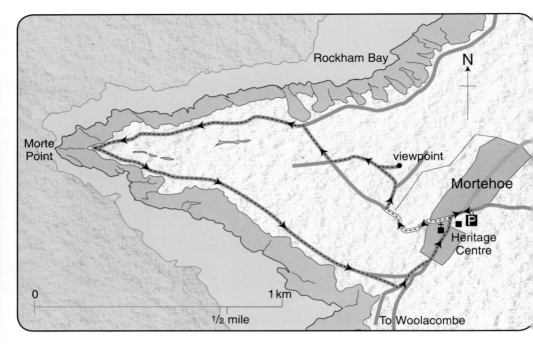

Walk 9 Mortehoe and Morte Point

Distance: 4 km (2 1/2 miles)
Character: Choose a clear day for this stimulating coastal walk: the views are superb, especially from Morte Point with its dramatic rock formations. There is one short sharp ascent, and rough footing in places.

Turn left out of Mortehoe car park and take the lane between the church and the 'Ship Aground' – its name indicating how dangerous this coast can be. The lane becomes a track. Stay with it as it passes to the right of the cemetery. Go through the iron gates ahead into Morte Point Memorial Park.

There are many paths in this area, and its easy to get confused, but they all lead in the end to Morte Point, so don't worry! About 20 m beyond the gates, turn sharp right uphill, signed VIEWPOINT.

Keep right at a path crossing, then bear left at the next junction. Turn right where a fingerpost points to the VIEWPOINT, from which there are magnificent views of Rockham Beach and Bull Point with its lighthouse.

Retrace your steps from the viewpoint and turn right, towards the point. When you reach a really broad grassy path, turn right on it,

20

downhill. Join the Coast Path (MORTE POINT). Keep right at a bench and follow the path to the Point.

The jagged Morte slates have claimed many ships, including five in the winter of 1852 alone. A later wreck was the SS *Collier*, 114 tons, which ran aground in 1914. She was one of the first steamships to carry mail from Australia; her anchor is displayed in front of the Ship Aground.

Continue on the Coast Path for 1.4km. At a point just below the houses, the path divides. Turn left, MORTEHOE, and follow the path steeply uphill. Join the lane and walk up into the village. Pass the 16th century stone and cob 'Chichester Arms', which has some fine sea pictures, to St Mary's. The church tower was built around 1270 and the little door into it was originally the church door. Also medieval is the tomb of William de Tracey.

Retrace your steps to the car park, where the Heritage Centre offers a cameo of local history. Shipwrecks, farming and tourism all feature, and there are interactive games for children.

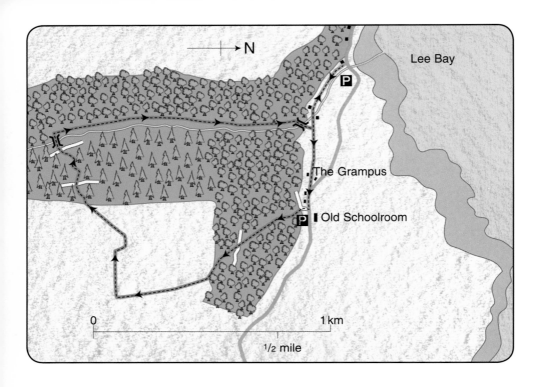

Walk 10   Lee and Borough Valley

Distance: 4 km (2 1/2 miles)

Character: Much of this walk is along woodland paths, giving welcome shade on hot days. Because of strong salt winds, woods are a rarity on the North Devon coast, where trees usually only grow to full height in sheltered places like Borough Valley. There is one longish climb to Windcutter Hill, and one steep descent to the woodland valley.

Start from the car park beside Lee Bay. (If this is full, there is an alternative car park by the Old Schoolroom craft gallery.) Join the driveway which runs inland to the right of the car park, becoming a footpath and passing the 'Grampus Inn'. This very attractive pub with low beamed ceilings and a pretty beer garden gets its name from creatures of the dolphin family.

Reaching a lane, continue ahead. Just beyond a red telephone booth (a threatened species!) and before the second car park, turn right on a driveway, then almost immediately left, PUBLIC FOOTPATH. Cross a stile, PUBLIC FOOTPATH WINDCUTTER HILL.

The path climbs steeply through trees to a vehicle track. Turn left,

22

then bear right on a woodland path, up to a kissing gate. Continue ahead through two fields with the hedge on your right.

At the far end of the second field, turn right, FOOTPATH TO BOROUGH VALLEY. Keep the hedge on your left . Cross a stile and continue ahead, then use the waymark posts to navigate over rough pasture and down to the far left corner of the field, where the path re-enters woodland by a stile.

Just 25 m ahead the path divides. Turn left, follow the path slightly uphill for 30 m, then right and downhill, to a forestry track. Turn right and immediately sharp left to continue downhill as signed. Use the yellow paint marks on the trees to follow the route. Cross another forestry track and continue downhill on the signed footpath.

Cross the stream by the footbridge and turn right. The path runs parallel to the stream. When it divides, continue ahead, PUBLIC FOOTPATH TO LEE. This leads gently downhill through mixed woodland to a path junction.

Turn right, PUBLIC FOOTPATH. Cross a footbridge and stile, then continue ahead with the wall on your right. Turn left and retrace your steps to the beach. The best view of Lee Bay and its rock strata is obtained by turning left up the lane for 100 m.

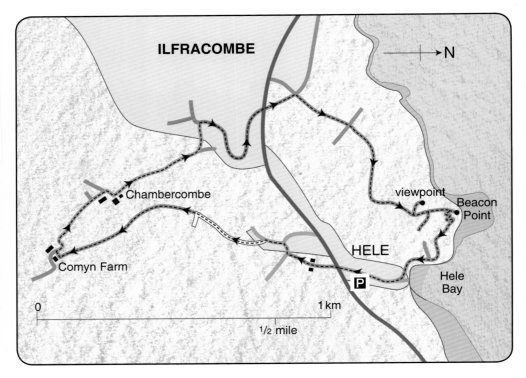

Walk 11   Hele and Chambercombe

Distance: 4km (2½ miles)
Character: This rewarding walk includes superb views of Ilfracombe, the coast, and Devon's chequerboard of green fields. It also passes Hele Mill and Chambercombe Manor, both well worth a visit. There is one long ascent and one long descent.

Turn left out of Hele Bay car park. Cross the main road carefully and take the PUBLIC FOOTPATH opposite, to Hele Mill. Continue on the footpath to a tarmac lane. Turn right, follow the lane around the bend and keep left, COMYN TRAYNE. At Witheridge Place, turn left up a tarmac track. Walk uphill to a left bend: take the PUBLIC FOOTPATH straight ahead at this point, which leads to Comyn Farm.

Entering the farmyard, turn right and right again, PUBLIC BRIDLEWAY ILFRACOMBE. Walk along this tarmac track or lane to Chambercombe Manor, then for a further 400m. Stay on the lane as it curves left to a road junction. Turn right, and follow the street as it winds round, then descends to the main road.

Cross carefully and take the tarmac path to the left of the swimming pool. After passing the pool turn right and follow the tarmac path uphill to another junction. Continue ahead, COAST PATH TO HELE BEACH, and climb to the coast path's highest point. Divert left here to a viewpoint with information board on the 114 m summit.

Retrace your steps to the Coast Path and turn left. Ignore a right turn. You'll reach an old viewing platform. From here the path zigzags downhill to another junction. Turn left at the Coast Path waymark. Turn right at the beach, back up the road to the car park.

Hele Mill (limited seasonal opening) is mentioned on a map of 1525, but the present corn mill is of unknown age. Derelict after 1945, it was restored in the 1970s and is run as a working museum with an attractive tea garden.

Chambercombe Manor's tearooms and beautiful gardens (donations) are open to the public, as are the woodland walks. It began as a medieval open hall house and has been continuously occupied over the centuries. There are fascinating guided tours, introducing visitors to the chequered and sometimes tragic past of Chambercombe, and the ghosts said to haunt it.

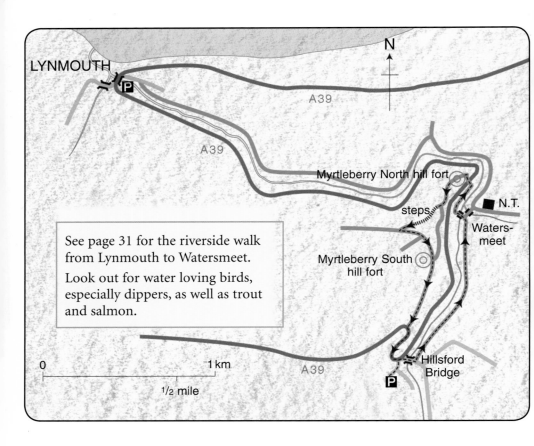

N

LYNMOUTH

A39

A39

Myrtleberry North hill fort

steps

N.T.

Waters-meet

Myrtleberry South hill fort

See page 31 for the riverside walk from Lynmouth to Watersmeet.

Look out for water loving birds, especially dippers, as well as trout and salmon.

0   1 km

A39

Hillsford Bridge

1/2 mile

Walk 12   Hillsford Bridge and Watersmeet

Distance: 3.25 km (2 miles)

Character: An excellent riverside and ridge walk by well-marked foot-paths, with dramatic views. One long steep ascent, relieved in part by steps.

Start from the National Trust's Combe Park car park – entrance just to the west side of Hillsford Bridge. Leave the car park and turn right over Hillsford Bridge, then turn left, PUBLIC BRIDLEWAY WATERSMEET. Approaching Watersmeet, turn left down steps to a wooden foot-bridge, which gives a lovely view of the cascading river.

Divert to the right over a second footbridge to visit the National Trust shop, information centre and tearoom, housed in a former Victorian hunting and fishing lodge.

Retrace your steps over the bridges and follow the steep zigzag path uphill for 100 m. Turn right, LYNTON BARBROOK OVER THE CLEAVES. Cross the road ahead and continue uphill on the footpath, LYNTON LYNMOUTH VIA THE CLEAVES. The path climbs steeply to Myrtleberry North Iron Age enclosure, with its clearly defined ramparts.

Follow the steep path uphill. Ignore a left turn and continue up a flight of steps.

At a path junction, turn sharp left, MW HILLSFORD BRIDGE. Pause to recover your breath and enjoy the marvellous views across the cleaves and over the sea to Wales, but spare a thought for the gallant Lynmouth lifeboat crew. One January night in 1899 they were requested by telegraph to assist the *Forrest Hall*. Unable to launch from Lynmouth because of high seas, they hauled their heavy lifeboat more than 22 km over the 400 m high hills opposite you, with only the aid of horses, and launched from Porlock to aid the stricken vessel and her crew.

Follow the path past Myrtleberry South Iron Age enclosure. Continue ahead, HILLSFORD BRIDGE. On reaching the main road, turn left downhill, then right into the car park.

More really short walks

Here are some excellent walks which are either not circular, or don't require much explanation or a map.

13 Speke's Mill Mouth

The 1.25 km (³/₄ mile) of path between Hartland Quay (Walk 2) and the South West Coast Path's largest waterfall at Speke's Mill Mouth offers some of Devon's most spectacular coastal scenery in return for a fairly modest effort. The vista along the cliffs and far into Cornwall is stunning (photo above). On the way there are marvellous rock formations, both in the cliffs and in the rocky beaches below, especially at Speke's Mill Mouth, accessed by steps.

14 Clovelly

Clovelly is a historic fishing village built into a steep valley along a cobbled and stepped path, still traversed by donkeys and sleds rather than motors. It has many attractions, including its little harbour and its visitor centre. Having paid for admission, you may add to the pleasure of your visit by exploring the Coast Path eastwards along Hobby Drive from the top of the village. Nearly 5 km (3 miles) long, Hobby Drive was part of a 19th century landscaping scheme by the wealthy Hamlyns of Clovelly Court. It makes a superb walk.

15   Upper Tamar Lake

The Tamar Lakes lie on the border between Devon and Cornwall, south of Clovelly, between Bradworthy and Kilkhampton. A permissive path circles the Upper Tamar Lake, which is used for fishing and sailing. The facilities include car park, toilets and seasonal café. The circuit is 5km (3 miles) – just cross the dam and turn left around the lake. It can be muddy. Generally it's good for wildlife once you're away from the watersports centre.

16   Saunton Sands

From Saunton Sands car park it is possible to walk for up to 6km along the golden beach, one of Devon's finest seaside walks. You may wish to add an exploration of Braunton Burrows. A huge area of sand dunes, the Burrows are a UNESCO Biosphere Reserve noted for flowering plants, butterflies and birds. Please note that whilst the public is generally very welcome on the Burrows, part is also used as a military training area. On rare occasions, red flags are flown and this area is closed for live firing. You may see soldiers or military vehicles – keep out of their way and don't touch any debris.

17 Croyde and Baggy Point

The well surfaced and gently graded footpath from the National Trust car park to Baggy Point provides excellent coastal views. Fascinating formations of shale and sandstone, plus varied birdlife, including colonies of gulls as well as raptors and larks, add to the interest.

18 Hele to Watermouth

The Coast Path between Hele and Watermouth offers some of the most magnificent views of Exmoor's high cliffs. Leave your car at the roadside car park 500 m east of Hele on the main road and follow the Coast Path. At first it runs parallel to the road, but happily turns seaward to Rillage Point and on to Widmouth Head, a superlative viewpoint (photo above).

19 Heddon's Mouth Cleave

A beautiful level path, 1.7 km (1 mile) long, links the National Trust car park and the beach at Heddon's Mouth. Cut by a fast flowing river, Heddon's Mouth Cleave is a steep sided valley lined by towering cliffs rising to 248 m (818 ft). Turn left out of the car park and left in front of Hunter's Inn, COMBE MARTIN BARNSTAPLE. After 300 m, turn right, HEDDON'S MOUTH.

Simply ignore all side turnings and follow the path to the beach. Retrace your steps for 200 m. Turn left over the footbridge and follow the river back to Hunter's Inn.

20 Lynton North Walk

This level tarmac walk offers superb views along the coast and over the sea to Wales. It bridges Lynton's gravity driven cliff railway (1890) and can be continued to the exceptional Valley of Rocks, a distance of 2 km (1 1/4 miles). Start by facing the parish church and turning left NORTH WALK HILL LEADING TO NORTH WALK.

21 Lynton Hollerday Hill

The lofty views of the Foreland and the Valley of Rocks from Hollerday Hill's viewpoint (244 m) richly repay the climb. Take the footpath HOLLERDAY HILL to the right of Lynton's exuberantly Victorian Town Hall and Tourist Information Centre.

Follow the path as it winds uphill. Continue uphill HOLLERDAY HOUSE and uphill at the next junction SUMMIT VALLEY OF ROCKS. Continue to VIEWPOINT, perched on an Iron Age settlement, for the view in the photograph below.

22 Lynmouth to Watersmeet

The dramatic riverside path from Lynmouth to Watersmeet (2.5 km/ 1 1/2 miles) winds through a deep wooded valley. Beautiful at any time, it is doubly so after rain when the East Lyn roars over tumbled boulders and its several waterfalls are supercharged. Please beware of slippery rocks and avoid this walk after very heavy rain – the river rises extremely fast and can be dangerous. See page 26 for map.

Park at Lyndale Cross car park in Lynmouth. Cross the road bridge at the lower end. Turn right along Tors Road and walk uphill, parallel to the East Lyn. After 100 m, bear right through a public garden and follow the bankside route WATERSMEET.

The National Trust tea-garden awaits you!

Other North Devon and Exmoor walks books from Bossiney Books

Shortish walks – north Devon (6-8 km)
Shortish walks on Exmoor (6-9 km)
North Devon Pub Walks (8-18 km)
Exmoor Pub Walks (8-15 km)

We also publish walks books covering the whole of Devon and Cornwall and much of Somerset: please see our website, www.bossineybooks.com